You Can Almost
Hear Their Voices

by

K. V. Skene

Indigo Dreams Publishing

First Edition: You Can Almost Hear Their Voices

First published in Great Britain in 2010 by:
Indigo Dreams Publishing
132 Hinckley Road
Stoney Stanton
Leics
LE9 4LN

www.indigodreamsonline.com

ISBN 978-1-907401-10-7

British Library Cataloguing in Publication Data. A CIP record for this book can be obtained from the British Library.

Designed and typeset in Times New Roman by Indigo Dreams.

Cover design by Ronnie Goodyer at Indigo Dreams.

Printed and bound in Great Britain by Imprint Academic, Exeter.

For Christopher, Florida and Samantha,
Allyson and Martin
and always and forever
for Leigh

CONTENTS

trying to solve the mystery of ourselves,
our children, theirs...

and the sea with all her teeth and tentacles,
swallows the sun in defiance

as we count the seconds to thunder,
anticipate rain.

You Can Almost Hear Their Voices

trying to solve the mystery of ourselves,
our children, theirs...

BECOMING FAMILIAR
BECOMING NEW

power lines sing themselves to sleep

streetlights fumble for shadows

the splayed paws of rain
warm whisper of wind
and magnolia dapple the darkening grey

a tame traffic light, a black and white night
up ahead a tidy playground
folds itself up

a small city becoming comfortable
                    becoming yours

AT WOODSGIFT

Light shivers from sky to blind window,
ripples the Lee,
interrupts our early morning tea
and apathy. A pair of mallards slip past –
too fast for reflection. The heron stares
down. Upstream something has happened,
the long brown river races,
chases its own dappled-by-spring-blossoms song
that dark rivers, like this one, need
to carry on.

CORCAIGH

It's the greenness of it, its wolfhound howlings; the black humour laid over eight hundred years of history. It's the smooth Irish whisky lost-in-translation prose propped by the side of the road announcing future deconstructions. It's the way voices call out to each other like soft birds answering other birds-of-a-feather all at once and how, unless you know who you are, you don't know where to look. It's the storm-sodden trees, leaves fat and dripping, the moss-mellowed stonewalls and railings and overabundance of wild fuchsias, God's Tears, edging the gritty streets. It's the Crayola shops and B&Bs along Western Road with up-to-the-minute cars inching, bumper to bumper, to Ballincollig and beyond; the shy pair of black swans circling the Loch; the schools of silver mullet struggling up the shallow Lee at end of summer, the myriad of wayside shrines and St. Finbarre's trumpeting angel. It's the high way Sunday's Well takes us home.

AFTER A POETRY READING AT TIGH FILÍ

Mindfull (I can never listen fast enough.)
after the pipes, the red wine and the craic,
and the buzz that always follows
as if the blind suddenly saw, the dumb
found voice,
I walk into a wide-eyed summer evening.
MacCurtain, stressed out on prosody,
couldn't share a word
so I turn down, over St Patrick's,
watch the buskers
play up their sprung rhyme, plum lines
to pull the punters.
Grand Parade and Washington
dig concrete and confessionals, push
brown bags of how-do-I-love-thee lyrics
and lite (no fat) verse. Take my own time
with Lancaster Quay, read the polyphonic Lee,
scan its burnished mirror-surface, listen
to the rush of shadow on stone –
it's old and it's cold and
I'm drunk on riverwater as well as words
(and wine). I cross my heart
but no more bridges,
pass the wrought iron gates of UCC
and its instructive deconstructions.
Mindless (I can never fly high enough.)
I hit Western
and like a sated she-bear
slouch towards home.

UNDER AN AMPHIBIOUS SUN

Spit-sodden clouds overlook
the obsessive deconstruction of Eyre Square;
the downtown glare of shops,
pubs, colour-blind cafés
littered with leftover lunchers,
cellphones 'on'.
Everything vibrates
like stones on a sea-stunned beach.
Everyone's smooth, sleek, sumptuous,
is look-at-me
staring into tomorrow
like the gulls that take up sky, shake
down Galway – their waterlogged reflections
no longer on hold. In no time
each spin-dry dialler
pulls an overstriped umbrella,
fakes an all-important call
and rain's the only thing allowed to fall.

APRIL AND THE SUN

As April and the sun repaint old skies
a newer blue, hang birdsong everywhere,
a mallard's mirror cracks, a cockerel's cries
sets unsung wings to thrumming – here... No, there...

Then April and the wind run lover's lane,
smite blackthorn blossoms, bite brightbudding leaves
from weeping willows, spike the catkin's cane,
pull perfect petals off magnolia trees

and spill them on the millpond just like ice-
bergs, while rainbows submarine its weedy deeps.
April rains too hard, too imprecisely,
and overruns the millrace – hide-`n-seeks

behind the wrought-iron gates where justborns lie
awaiting May`s laburnum lullaby

ON THE FIRST SUNDAY AFTER THE FIRST FULL MOON AFTER THE VERNAL EQUINOX

under the clarity of too much sky,
we stop
to witness the arrival
of too much light, ribbons of it
roll over the somnolent hills –
a beacon, an omen, a bird
flying –
kissing the morning awake
and we look
for simple answers – in the landscape,
in our not-so-perfect past,
in a sun sign
trying to solve the mystery of ourselves,
our children, theirs...
and we listen
for names, for the cut-in-solid-rock
ogham of things:
carraig, cist, cloch fháda...
stones and bones in our mouths
and we are dumb
for a moment and for a moment
we have only the rite
and remain silent
under the clarity of too much love.

carraig – rock
cist – cairn/grave
cloch fháda – long stone
ogham – Celtic tree alphabet

ALIVE, ALIVE, OH!

Rain. We deplane, puddle onto #41 bus, off
at Mountjoy Square. "Cross the street
turn left at the light". Bed,
breakfast, umbrella and out

into traffic – greyer, grittier
than we ever imagined. Construction cranes,
cathedrals, statued O'Connnell,
Parnell, even sweet Molly Malone

coax our camera. Across the dark Liffey,
gapes greystoned Trinity. Ssssshhh, we ghost
between a golden past
and our not-so-shiny future. The face

of this city is old. It grew old
long ago – but no wiser. Hand in hand
down Grafton we dodge students, shoppers
and far more dedicated tourists. End

in green St. Stephen's Green, breathless,
as all the city children
merry-go-round us faster
and faster.

YOU CAN ALMOST HEAR THEIR VOICES

cutting through the tired traffic-hum. All at once
summer children have taken over Dublin,
the streets singing and you're fumbling for the words.
Unburdened and beautiful in their skins, as you once were –
no history, no guilt, no regrets, no bloodshot flush of roses,
heavy-scented and blowsy –
just before evening caught you and your excuses
out on the terrace, out in the jangling air
you would share with everyone. Your hands, steady as always,
pour sweet wine into the best long-stemmed glasses,
place bowls of strawberries and ice cream
on the white table,
prop the French doors wide, inviting
forgotten friends, the ghosts of innumerable June brides
out into the garden, still damp with summer rain
and madly overgrown.

AGAIN

light gathers
as dreams gather
at the edge of sight. You are

a child
hide-and-seeking (at the milk-tooth
and cow-lick stage). Too soon
the surrounding air, soft as a moth wing,
darkens
like any act of love. You are

under the rose,
have no idea of tomorrow
in your head – pinned
by that rapier-thin ache/
ecstasy
you had almost forgotten. Night breaks

into the corners of your eyes.
Last call for the innocent
who still insists
on happily-ever-after. You are

in love,
the sun sinks into the purple hour,
out of time
out of your mind
again.

PIANISSIMO

In the small hours
when no one else is listening

you feel the shape of your hands
as your fingers open

empty as the house
when your mother is not home

                    is nowhere
she can be touched or spoken to

and you in your second-best dress
cherry-red sandals

alone at the Bechstein
flames playing over your hands

even as you hold note on note
her song

dying. It is beautiful
and so are you

with your pupils wide open as mirrors
the music inside beckoning.

SING TO THE CHILD

Voice of a mother I almost remember,
green spring of Ireland – how fast you can die,
sing to the child left bloodstained forever.

Teach only love songs (hate will take longer)
after the first death, the last lullaby.
Voice of a mother (I almost remember

wounds you kissed better) tell of a brother,
ripe red his birth-blood on your dead white thigh.
Sing for the child left bloodstained forever,

suckle your first-born, fat with night-terrors,
breast milk and blarney soon won't satisfy.
Voice of a mother I almost remember,

speak of the lives all women surrender
(your daughter died in my daughter's birth-cry)
sing of the child left bloodstained forever

mourning her life, soft-mouthed while her lover
promises rebirth. I know how he lies.
Voice of a mother I almost remember,
sing with the child left bloodstained forever.

TRAD MUSIC NIGHT AT SIN É

A soft evening, windows blur
as we circle sidewalk smokers,
slide in, let the music roll,

bounce off wallfuls of postcards, photos,
out-of-date adverts, a John Lennon poster, a limp
Cuban flag and an oversized oil of a haggard hurler,

semi-lit by a collection of kitchen candles
jammed into bottles, counterpoint
to our empties and elbows...

A fiddle spins out a reel, *allegro,*
just this side of reckless,
followed by banjo, bodhrán, guitar

while the pipes play along, segue into another
till a tin whistle mellows
the mood

and a girl sings
in a voice of country, sacrifice, loss
as if she had already drifted away...

ONE PER PERSON

We are who we are
the day we are born, we live
at the appropriate distance

in a stone-faced town
where kids collect in corners
like sheep

and houses hold together
long enough
for closets to fill with familial bones

and dissidents rumble down alleyways
brushing up our fears
until we ID

our dear departing – the high-heeled girl
clattering by
every Friday night, the drunk,

tearing at his thin shirt,
as he bleeds
into the street. We don't plan this –

it just happens. The death rate remains
one per person
and everyone wants to believe

they'll be missed.   Other people's lives
are never as real
as we want them to be. Tonight,

lying by your side, I confess
I made you up. Trust me.
No one will notice.

THE OPPOSITE OF TRUTH
(Bishop Lucey Park)

Hope is green in the early morning,
patterned with the shadow-lace
of trees. Prayer is this
time of day
and meets itself
on a damp park bench
to watch water spiral
a surreal sculpture of verdigris
leaves
and flying geese – useless
as a politician's promise, dull
as an unspent cent.
This is a place that says
nothing but thinks
green, flaunts
green, insists
everything is possible.
Everything.
Even tomorrow.

AFTER THE ANGELUS

silence
the window blind and blank
February rain outside the pane
cold beyond comforting
still I hold your heart and hope
in my helpless hands
and let you go

OUTWARD AND VISIBLE SIGNS
divination by the lines and swellings of the hand

i. interpreting the runes impressed in each palm at birth

She arrives, on time,
an uncertain thirty-something clutching
her shopping and scans the room
surreptitiously. She's left him
back in their cramped flat,
smoking, trying to read the paper,
the three-year old
hobbyhorsing his leg, the baby
whimpering... This is a mixed hand,
a square, practical palm
with the long, flexible fingers of a dreamer.
Its shibboleths of marks and loops,
its healing striate, its logic
apparent in tapered finger phalanxes,
(arch on the thumb, peacock eye
on the Mercury finger). Here's
the significator for marriage, a love affair, an abortion,
an accident. Here's a star on the Mount of Jupiter,
trident on the Mount of Apollo, grille
on the percussion edge...

ii. the girdle of Venus

Follow the fine line from Jupiter to Mercury
and back again – find love
before it begins to fade, before life begins to wobble
like a fledgling.

        She sees herself as in a photograph,
younger, slimmer, sexier, snug in blue jeans
sitting on the grass near a lake,
talking to her lover.
                Older hands
are rarely so full of promise.

iii. a ring of Solomon

Curled under the Jupiter finger
its presents enhances
every possible position. *Of course*

she's played this game before
but now a life is in her hands
and she's looking for a way out,

a release from disbelief. So many excuses
can be held in the mouth like an egg,
neither sweet nor sour nor

unbreakable
and are left unspoken for years
before they dissolve into the matrix,

families brought to the brink,
where only the speaker is real
saying what is usually unsayable...

iv. an island in the life line

Of course you were never at home there,
you drifted into it and it was so empty, so quiet
you started talking, really talking;
told him your dream, went beyond
the all-too-familiar; opened your hands, filled
your mouth, your body... *Caught up in confessions,*
she's a child running downhill, skirt flying –
her heart with it. Now, the affair over, dead
up ahead, you don't care who loved most,
who lied first and want to stop
spilling milk, beans, intimate secrets, innocent blood
and why you want this is written in your hand
but you don't want to believe it.
That's written there too.

v. a branched head line

Years afterwards you may wonder
what might have been
had you held on

and a late afternoon sun sprawls
wall to wall –
she looks up

as a red balloon hangs over the quiet street
strung to a small fist. Yourself
stubbornly still, the air rarefied

and a small bluebottle batters
the windowpane –
she doesn't see

while nothing makes you live more intensely
than learning what has to happen
after the law of gravity kicks back in

and her scruffy Sierra waits
by the back gate –
he doesn't know she's here.

vi. a mystic cross

A cross on the Plain of Mars
opens the narrow gate between substance
and illusion. You will be blinded
by unreason, specious facts,
the obscene images of a delusional age,
by something that is not love
but knows its gestures
and even if evening brings cool oblivion
morning always comes
and out you must go – *like that little girl*
with scabs on her knees
peeking out from behind mommy's legs,
pulling little girl faces at the world.
Not extraordinary after all…

vii. the widow's line

Reaching up under the Mount of Mercury,
a tear ready
to fall. *Suddenly she's overtired,*
her full breasts are leaking
and she's anxious to go – before
whatever's left of her youth smothers
in overstuffed rooms, shivers in doorways
inhaling wet cigarettes
in the rain and the shoulders of her dead
hang in the closet like second-hand skins
and glass after glass spills and
the flat smells of cat and takeaway dinners
for one
and mourning spreads its brown stain
over the carpet. Before
there's no stopping it...

vii. the bracelets of life

Three parallel lines, three
well-defined rascetts twisted firmly
around each wrist, permanently
scarring each blue vein as it surfaces
amid a fragility of nerve, muscle, tendon,
brittle bone. Let another's heart
beat beneath your fingertips as regular
as a riptide, smile at the children
who circumnavigate your city, learn to speak
their language. *Before she steps out the back door*
she hesitates – still wants to be told
she will win a lottery, fly oceans, continents,
meet a perfect stranger who will tell her
she is beautiful,
so she can love him for it...
Here is water you can walk on, a full glass
offered up before your aging eyes – before
the inevitable blackholes implode upon your retinas
like unacknowledged wishes, like
collapsing stars.

and the sea with all her teeth and tentacles,
swallows the sun in defiance.

AFTER COLUMBUS

christened them 'Las Tortugas',
spying shoals of sea turtle,
Sir Francis Drake
(another literal minded sailor)
renamed these low-slung isles
for their crocodiles.

Cayman stuck,
although the turtles survived (barely)
and the crocs didn't.

Settled by shipwreck survivors,
deserters, debtors, the occasional pirate,
(Blackbeard, Ann Bonney)
a few transplanted Jamaicans
(with and without slaves)

and despite swarms of mosquitoes,
nests of ticks, pods of cowitch,
'East End fish babies' built,
went down to the sea in ships
of Cayman mahogany, laden
with thatch palm rope, sarsaparilla,
cotton, fish
and turtle

and slow-stepped (in island-time)
from a staging post
for elsewhere bound schooners
to a 'Love Boat' drop
for sun-bored, sea-sick, born-to-shop sailors,
credit card in hand –

buy a time-share on Seven Mile Beach,
duty-free in George Town, 'mudslides'
at Rum Point,
and postcards from Hell.

THIS ISLAND

is a heavyweight of sun
on burnt shoulders; a cool nor'wester
massaging
your back.

is salt on your tongue; grit
between your teeth; the scent
of morning glory
after rain

and sand shifting underfoot.

is a blueblade horizon;
a red ball of sun
that blinks
green

and leg-aching nightmares
double parked
in one hot bed
after another

and the sound of steel drums

is heartpound, bellyflutter,
a stubborn slowbrainworm
digging
the dark

till the white, white moon
smiles
and smiles
and follows you home

and you are beautiful tonight.

A RED SUN BURNS

down the neither-here-nor-there hour
at the edge of evening
and I hear night talking
in a voice
whose accent outwits the Caribbean,
recalls the cold, cold winds
of Canada. Tonight
the shadows under my eyes
look like bruises
on the moon. Outside the dark
drums, cool and liquid,
and the sea sounds
of strummed steel. Insect
tears gather to listen,
yearn to belong. Bit by bit
my heart breaks
and night speaks to me
in its own language
of black – soft, scented syllables
that say I have changed,
have become another person – older,
more vulnerable,
yct more alive
than I ever imagined possible
and I wonder
as I turn from the window,
smile
(but not for the party-people)
how far I dare go,
how fast,
before I have to come
home.

IF YOU STAND

on the balcony's edge
you will hear the sh-sh-sh-sh
of sea
on sand and the windbirds
whistle
in
heart
of palm
and a cricket's
thin scream,
green
as the grass
moonshadowed
three floors below. You can hear
it all
at once
and there is a reason
for nightlistening
only small children
know – the beat
        beat
        beat
of blood
in your veins, the breath
in your bird-hollow bones,
the yank on the string
that holds you to earth
as you
and this island
slow-gather
yourselves
to sleep.

STEEL DRUMS

hum under the bougainvillea –
iced rum, cool slice of shadow
before sleep. You speak

of distant dreams,
slip love-notes
in between breathing. Suddenly

the pit-pat of rain
and a small wind shouts
out of loneliness. We touch,

our hand soft, as if
our bruises showed. The night
drums on and on

and over us (wild wings
on sounding waves). Everyday
the sky arcs

higher and higher. Everynight
stars fall
into the sea – the deep blue

we live by and would not change
if we could. Awake
the pale moon (faint

as a mourning widow) whispers
what could be half-a-hymn
a prayer

at the skin of evening. Steel
drums wrap old lovers, like us,
in a siren song – sly

                    as a woman.

THE BIG EMPTY

After the sun's red ball
falls over the edge
of the world
the big empty
mind of the sky
deepens, deepens
until you are sucked
into its black
unforgiving – no shape,
no solidity, no certainty,
just the warm breath
of white frangipani
floating on air,
the half-remembered voice
of someone loved
when love was wasted...

A backward step,
a long embrace
and the last door out
closes against you
and there is only the waiting –
the coin-toss, the crap-shoot
of a heart on the brink –
and barely there, barely heard
a nightbird, hidden
in shadow, hidden
in wind.

BLACKSKINNED TROPICAL NIGHTS

bronze cocoplum, purple sea grape,
poisonous ackie – I grow fat
on dark Caymanian dreams. Snowpale

in temperate zone skin,
I twist stubborn joints, fold spine,
bend as the hot sea sucks

up the moon. Blackcoral bastard
vision, green turtle song
of wrongs – Hell's open for business

one mile up the road. Shut
on Sundays.

AND YOU SLEEP

in the sheltered cove of childhood,
clear as rainwater,
a thin sheet of silence
spread over you

the sky, a guilty handprint,
clenches – knuckles an old green-grey,
so bruised
it hurts to see

behind the bones of dead casuarina,
palm, breadfruit, an obliteration
of galaxies, the blind eye
of a moon,

a sea
whose serpent mouth
sucks the kisses out of you
with a roar

you drop down, down, down
into Black Durgon Sound – until dawn
breaks through
and you wake,

the taste of blue
all over you.

BEFORE

the southern sun slipped out of the sea
you said love is a foreign country
and you don't speak the language,
peace is that split second
it takes to reload and monarchs
need no reason for being
butterflies...
                    ...and I said,
high in the sky a sliver of moon
shines without shadow,
the bedroom smells of candles
just before they sputter out.
I have come from Canada
and I can go back home
where morning will break
without you
as before.

AN APPEARANCE OF PELICANS

From a sullen sky a pair of pelicans
collapse wide, wide wings and drop
into our blue-grey day.
With a quick flick of white underfeathers
they settle, long beaks to breasts,
and their round, brown bodies take over
our scene.

The surf slides them apart, together, apart...
Abruptly he hurls his bulk over her,
belly to back – one creature,
four flailing wings.
They separate,
drift for a moment, then lift and slalom
out of sight.

And we are alone again, on a beach,
searching a louring sky,
an uncertain sea
on an island where heaven opens,
pours down happiness
secret and wild,
as sudden as laughter.

A PELICAN SKY

dips long dun feathers deep into the tide
that rakes the beach, anticipates the rain.
Sandcrabs zig-zag through salt-foam in their side-
ways run for home – I can't go home again,
home's not the same. Two pelicans lift-off
to choreograph the heavyweight of air
and share their heart-beat music – a lofty
pas de deux pour l'hiver. Everywhere
the same rain rains, the wind begins a hymn
to loneliness, to loss, to whatever might
have been. This long, last night is dropping in
to strum the brain-stem, shiver small candlelight.
Open the window, open wide the sea,
open the wind's wings and let them fly me.

GEORGE TOWN IN THE RAIN

as the sky, down on its knees,
surrenders,

whitewashes the out-of-context office blocks
we borrowed tomorrow from and never returned,

scrubs Sounds & Things, shuts Divers Down,
drowns Chicken!Chicken! and, neurotic

as a nor'easter, jumps the traffic light
(the only stop in town)

as sirens shake up the outskirts, overspill
the empty harbour, the childless park,

(faithless as sky to sea, to ship,
to scrubbed ironshore)

where loners and losers stumble,
eye the myopic scene and nothing,

nothing becomes smaller, sharper,
just bigger, blurrier, out of focus

as last season's lover – longed for
and long gone.

WET

Step out of sight, of your shoes,
straight into crystallite surf.
Open your shirt, button
             by button
             by button –
black beads in a rosary.
Unbuckle belt, unzip zipper
and you're knee-deep and naked and in
for a swim – a new-born,
a child seeking baptism,
seeking to wash away
the touch of another, the sin
of believing, of bargaining
with memory (with god). Water.
A prayer,
a blessing, a caressing
rain
in a desert
as seeds green the pale sand
and wildflowers bloom
in the most barren of wombs.

UNDER THE MENISCUS

Silence is the secret,
the last secret –
nothing but breath-hiss as you hang
alive and hungry.
The old leatherback in your brain,
born in a colder sea,
lies in wait
for the smell of something once familiar,
for the first taste of it.

chromis, cottonwick, glasseye, snapper,
barjack, Spotted drum, gar, schoolmaster.

Like bright beads strung on a silver chain,
small fish slip in and out the deep holes
in the battered reef (seeking shelter,
subsistence) and ignore the obvious
gap between what was
and what is
that grows wider, deeper, emptier
in the cold motherhands
of the sea.

bigeye, spanish grunt, nurse shark, graysby,
trunkfish, rock beauty, jackknife, coney.

The view is circumscribed,
refracted.
Arms-length under the meniscus,
it slides into focus,
coral-bright as the eye of a god
you can't trust,
absorbing light, colour, wind shadows,
drownings – a home not your own.
Sometimes you can taste the salt.

highhat, black durgeon, sergeant major,
spotted eagle ray, blue tang, grouper.

Breaking through,
a billion threads of light
web the ocean,
strobe the surf-detritus
of her dead and dwindling children.
Suspended (weightless, shapeless)
you rock
and the sea, with all her teeth and tentacles,
swallows the sun in defiance.

dusky squirrelfish, fairy basslet,
porkfish, triggerfish, indigo hamlet.

Out of the unseeable deep,
spirals of silver
turn and turn and turn and turn
around you.
The sea-heart beating, beating
your first rhythm,
a flood-tide in the spine,
an ache you feel,
the bloody marrow in your bones.

stoplight, parrotfish, harlequin bass,
goatfish, barracuda, creole wrasse.

You are here,
falling in love with everything there is,
with no one at all.
Sometimes it's easier to exist falling,
turning in the tide
like a foetus in the womb,
the last sea-turtle
swimming. Swimming
alone, alone, alone, alone.

blackbar, soldierfish, hind, green moray,
hogfish, scrawled filefish, southern stingray.

SEVEN DAYS AND SIX NIGHTS OUT OF CONTEXT

Somewhere you've never been and yet

how wantonly the language elides
sanitised syllables, celebrates
familiar high days and holidays
as if you could really belong, be
careless of dirt,
dysentery, mindless of danger,
of losing your money/
your life as you open
to the beautiful strangers
casing Bodden Street, eyes
scanning slipshod shops,
bars, Saturday night's special
offers and you – too eager to clock in
or out of all the wrong places...

You hear the sound of laughter

as the blue sea spreads its light
to the horizon and Sunday
discovers the beach
and you descend, singularly aware
of cohabitating couples, absorbed
in each other
in a way that excludes and you're convinced
you will never have, never
love
anyone in that indelible way –
thigh touching thigh – yet
he looked at you. Looked.
At you.
And you became beautiful.

Someone somebody can love

because you've woken late, naked and
folded over another – Monday's
already full of firsts. Never again
can you pretend love
is only child's play, can you
deny why you overachieve, can you
blot out loneliness
with tequila shooters and a sullen
superiority. Last night
has to mean something, has to
mean more than the words you never heard
spoken before
by a still-lying-beside-you lover. Has to.
Has to.

After your first sea dance

you sleepwalk to sunset, steel drums
and the surfsounds
of laughter. You want love
to take you further, float you
through Tuesday, the whole island
your present: casuarina, hibiscus, the ocean
a blue intrusion, a free-for-all
as midnight falls
over the room you leave each morning
and two bodies fight the tide of two glossologies
as you swim unstable depths
where the questions you've not asked,
the ones that have no answers,
school...

So far whatever you wanted was given

and afterwards you breakfast on the balcony:
pomegranate juice, croissants, coffee
hot and black and bitter, the sun
bulging on the horizon as Wednesday
heaps too much honey in the spoon. It's early yet
it's still too late. Too late
to undo anything, to pretend *amour*
got lost in translation
when even the bruised clouds
fist as forecast, even the sea snarls
and you hold on to his hand
holding on to love
you count money,
the most important thing in his world.

The last place you want to be

as gulls pencil the air, scribble obscenities
like storm, like hurricane,
your heart emptier, thinner
than this glass
and you cannot cry
as you cross the boardwalk
Thursday's price tags flutter and children
and old women and tattooed strangers
reach for your money
stepping on toes
already blistered and swollen
as your belly and suddenly
the sky is falling
with unimaginable insistence.

Love is something that did not happen

without you the clock's hands cross and
only the taxi waits
and Friday headlines feature
yesterday's gale
and the storm-torn trip to the airport
passes in silence
and you think how you sought the whirlwind of it,
bought the full force of it, the madness,
the badness,
how he laughed and lied and left, how
the sky underneath you is blue,
your Bloody Mary is red
and you're flying... love
is something that did not happen at all.

as we count the seconds to thunder,
anticipate rain.

IN OUR HOUSE

bedrooms shift as we sleep, open
to blind hallways, grandfather
clock tick-tocks downstairs
the sofa slumps, the piano hums
Moonlight Sonata, our photographs
lie flat in their albums and grey cat
purrs over the pink velvet chair
as usual, we wake with white lilacs
on the round table, the cat licking its toes,
our daughter's long lashes, her brother

spins the piano stool, plays honky-tonk
and grey cat sniffs the pink velvet chair,
the wet lilacs, our photos slip from their pages,
slither under the sofa: dustballs, spiderwebs,
cookie crumbs, small faces smiling

TO WHOM IT MAY CONCERN

We live upstairs where voices are polite,
the sound of traffic muted. Shut
behind leaf-latticed brick, twelve tall windows
open for air and light. This is where
that regiment of road signs led
last March, the best of our lives jammed
in the old blue Metro, our eyes sunglassed
against the low sun. And we have learned
to love what is here, is essential
in the evolution of a house
into a home. So far
there have been no hauntings.
What was never to be mentioned
remains unsaid
and we have been given other signs to search for
along with the assurance
they don't exist.

EVERY HOUSE HAS A ROOM THAT DOESN'T EXIST

along with its more obvious architectural anomalies such as one-way
staircases and corridors that dead-end and demand a u-turn and
draughts with icicle fingers that reach under your shirt raising
gooseflesh and issues you don't want to deal with as insistent and
awkward as the briefcase you lug home each night full of urgent and
eyes-only papers you really can't be bothered to read and every house
has a drawer that locks with a key that is always down the crack in the
sofa or tucked behind somebody else's socks and every house has a
loft that is hard to enter and much too painful for its proportions which
gently gathers up the collateral damage of the choices you cling to
along with the dust and ashes of ancestral misjudgements while
reserving deep space for ongoing catastrophes and those nights
gulped down in haste under the grubby duvet of sad slow passion as
the year shifts its weight from one foot to another and the insistent
damp tugs at elbows and knees and every house embraces old lovers
and their cold-shouldered children beside the usual skinny nailbiters
judgmental ex-smokers preadolescent powerbrokers and one potential
murderer and every house keeps you cornered upstairs and down
sniffing out claustrophobic cubby-holes and closets hung with drop-
dead designerwear and mothballed skeletons but you have to believe
you're only looking for a small warm place to lie down in

WHAT YOU LEARN IN THE DARK

as the brain's votive candle
flickers beneath a holy picture,
spirals that covey of cut-glass angels
quick-frozen in flight;
as unforgiving as the harsh hiss
of overheated air in your lungs,
heavy drumroll of heartbeats,
hot blood flooding rubbery veins,
a sea-noise an ebb tide
and outside;
the underground thunder of trains,
dead silence of snow, of your overwound mind
unravelling this winter night,
its absence of colour, shape, solidity,
of beauty beneath the dry rot of regret
and the ache of acknowledging
you have been living someone else's death
for the longest time
and the only way out
                        is lonely.

AFTER THE LAST FUNERAL

We sat around one another
soaking in the June heat
of time together,
brothers and sisters improving
make-believe summers
climbing the apple trees – feeling,
as we did then,
father's soft and heavy hand
on our backs
pushing us forward into this future
and the fear of falling
out of childhood – its patterns
stamped on our skin, our genetic inheritance
leaves us defenceless,
we only know how to say nothing
and mean everything.
Lightning strokes the sky,
the streets shimmer – it's beautiful, this
the first city we all remember
leaving behind,
its geography now unfamiliar, its language
lumpen on our tongues
as we count the seconds to thunder,
anticipate rain.

IN A SECOND

the sun
shatters the double-glazing.
Outside,
a high-flying sky
cracks. Below,
the sea
sounds
cold. Child
of my childhood,
we share this grave
day-break,
hollow as a church
unserviced
overlong – I thank God
I no longer believe
in Him.

Spine folded
over the kitchen table,
you roll, light
a cigarette. Your words
smoke
before they're syllables,
your ache visible,
then gone... Child

of my carelessness,
we downshift
into a millennium
unanswerable as a prayer,
censured,
wrong – I thank God
I no longer need
to believe you.

We're waiting
for today to begin,
almost calmly
you exhale, your words
incense
in my kitchen,
(one last gasp from home)
my spongy lungs. "More tea?"

I whisper, squeezing in
between day/nightmares
I can almost see, almost
hear them beat their wings
hard against the pane,
almost believe
they're real and almost
mine.

BEEN THERE

way out there
a skittering shadow
scrambling
on the edge.

Passport, visa, ticket
and I'm doing time in a whisky-gilded lounge,
railway station,
bus stop –

heeding the pull of borderlines,
the checking in,
out
and never arriving...

as the scene shifts
with the language, with
the thrum of an engine's
blacknotes,

with the whitesound
of habitual highways
to places
I could be happy in.

You can fall in love
between hotel rooms
and dream of someone somewhere else –
I've been there,

way out there dying
for a fag and a Bloody Mary
to get me through till noon.
And I've done that,

bought the hair shirt
(redripe with stripes that scar my skin)
needing the pull of borderlines,
the going and going

and never arriving
home.

AND PEACE IS

slap-happy footprints criss-crossing a beach
under a sky as young as a yellow umbrella;
an old woman, cheeks crumpled with laughter,
feeding stale buns and fresh confessions to her pigeons;
a café on a street you fall in love with –
hot and bright and in-your-face
as an underground busker and peace is

a slow soggy jog in the rain, the lamps lit,
the small doors open to the night,
the square slabs of pavement solid underfoot;
a high-five from a giggle of schoolchildren
mudpuddling their way home and peace
is everything you wish for
when blowing out birthday candles and peace is

the understanding that comes between
birdsong and traffic pound; between
one heartbeat, and the next, and the next; between
a still small voice
and so many words of mass destruction and
peace is a beautiful stranger caught at a stoplight;
a fair-weather friend glimpsed across a crowded room;

the silence that shivers between
suicide bombers and retaliatory raids; between
sectarian skirmishes and pre-emptive strikes; between
those who kill and those who wait to be killed,
maimed, imprisoned, enslaved, left
stunned under a skewbald sky
that holds its breath and waits and waits and

a fey face behind a windowpane – there,
then gone.

FLYING WITHOUT YOU

Point of Departure   Heathrow, Charles de Gaulle, Cincinnati &
Northern Kentucky – a long, long way without
love – a word I can't live with
although I keep trying to. Touch me,
I bend. Kiss me, I open.
Want me,
I am warm air rising…

Gate 13   Even the clock disconnects
as minute by minute 747s
drop out of heaven,
howling,
as I wait (without you) to begin/
to be gone. The older I get
the more certain uncertainty is.

Take-off   And the earth turns around
its petrified past. I slip a ring
from my finger and take myself
(separately, deliberately)
into tomorrow – a detour, a début,
a divorce. Flying without you
is being unknown, uncared-for,
in an undiscovered country.

Suspended in Sky   Blue. The icecold blue
in which time disintegrates
and thoughts crystal upon conception.
The absolute bluenothingness that is tundra,
permafrost, glaciers smothered in wind,
slippery with snow-melt. The blueprint of a soul/
of a sea
in which wave after wave lifts, turns back
without looking.

Orbital Observation   Underneath our wings
a suicide sky. Inside my brain
there is no difference between falling
into everything and falling
into nothing
both leave you without a choice/
a prayer.

Re-entry   Without fanfare the earth rises,
the landscape expands
a little too fast: snowtrails, evergreen valleys,
skyhigh rivers slithering to sea
as small walleyed buildings shoulder
a switchblade highway, swell
to cityscape.

Touchdown   Flat earth and heavy bodyparts (Without you
I'm filling in the blanks with truths that aren't.)
and time restarts, slow-rolls the final runway,
as I lug my overweight carry-on,
my overwrought memories
out the designated door.

Grounded   Leaving Lester B. Pearson,
streetlights blink a downtown
tattooed in red and gold.
I know what I'm hoping for, holding
my breath for –
arriving (without you) at half-past Happy Hour –
I'll knock on that blue door on Bathurst Street
if without me
is the lonely place you want to be.

MIDAFTERNOON

the clocks thin hands
unfocus

unwind late winter light
work has emptied you

whoever you are
a stranger who could be a lover

another packaged tourist
with excess luggage

let me shelter you
for this unstable hour

keep the sun from your eyes
the weather

well behind the brink of
obsession

there is always a niagara
falling through everything we know

we'll take love as it comes
photographs of lost things

too small to matter
copper coins and buttons

the inconsequential bones of a cat
turn to ashes to dust to

dusk and the sun dies
from lack of attention

in the gloom your hands
your laughter down my spine

and hope seems as reasonable
as spring

A WOMAN CAN

live
through the end of the second thousand years,
dress her anorexia
in Versace,
catwalk city streets,

flash an orthodontic grin. Slip
out of set-up schemes, serialize
other women's husbands;
deride that merry-go-round
when the revolutions sicken.

breathe into the forgotten end
of phones, stand at weeping windows,
check into out-of-season,
out-of-luck
motels.

take winter walks under lampposts,
cold shoulders hunched
like hackles – fists
blue as the ice
she keeps her heart in.

grow old and into the mythology
of tall, dark, hand-me-down strangers
(half past their sell-by-date)
ready and willing
and unable...

double back to her bedsit, doublelock
the door, put on the gas,
out the Beaujolais
and watch the mantle clock
cover its white face with its hands.

tick tock tick tock tick
into another thousand years. A woman can
make up her mind, change her address.
A woman can
disappear.

AND SHE'S GONE WHERE SO MANY CHILDREN HAVE GONE

down roads we no longer recognize
without the words, the names of things
she's not yet heard, seen, smelt, used –
abused by the Fagin
who picks her up in a terminal
(bus? train? plane?)
drops her at the corner
and/or in a dumpster
with city-syllables
smeared on her lips, stuck
to the roof of her mouth,
caught in her throat like the words of a mother.

CAUGHT IN HER THROAT LIKE THE WORDS OF A MOTHER

gone mad, a father gone
down (Riding the blue bus
past doorways, subways, back alleys,
unshriven parks and public toilets
collapsing under their own dead weight.)
declaiming the syntax that soaks into pores,
the names that change everything: hooker
and hit, and coke and grass and fix
that (too quickly) feel familiar
and bearable and habitual and
business-as-usual
as finding the enemy dressed as love.

AS FINDING THE ENEMY DRESSED AS LOVE

as blue as an out-of-school sky, a holiday sea
and she's caught in city traffic,
embracing everything complex, messy,
riddled with coincidence
and she doesn't know how to decode street signs,
storefronts, headlines
and she can't read the streetwalkers, the pushers, the pimps,
the look-alike johns
(their eyes are inside, their words inaudible)
and she's their child, their vision, their voice
for too many things, too many big things
and she's gone where so many children have gone.

AND ONCE AGAIN

to lie through that last
December night, slow-shift

through endless cigarettes
and much too much red wine – drunk

and at home with disorderly,
(just another soft touch)

to whisper "yes,
yes again…"

backpage
a full calendar of resolutions – any

body at hand for *auld lang syne*
and once again

a year burns down
to its cold

and absolute
end.

It is the stars
The stars above us, govern our conditions.
Shakespeare (King Lear)

PALE STARS (IN THEIR DOTAGE)

♈
Aries　　　　Head on,
　　　　　　　eyes pebblewashed,
　　　　　　　cold and clear as springwater,
　　　　　　　edgy;

　　　　　　　a serious soul in suit and tie
　　　　　　　(shoes down at heel)
　　　　　　　out of humour – cash is quick,
　　　　　　　　　　　　love takes longer.

　　　　　　　It's the fear of explaining too much,
　　　　　　　not saying enough, that holds him back.
　　　　　　　Head high, a shoulder shrug,
　　　　　　　he'll charge,

　　　　　　　at a change of fortune,
　　　　　　　first sign of groundshift,
　　　　　　　to graze where the grass
　　　　　　　is greener

　　　　　　　and he won't give an inch,
　　　　　　　take a wider view,
　　　　　　　follow another – it's almost as if he was
　　　　　　　a brother of mine.

ठ
Taurus

Wrapped in second-hand fur, stubborn
dreams, she walks in, demands
love –

insists on mouth-to-mouth,
body part in body part
till the fun runs out

for everyone – her words shake
whatever holds your dreams
together,

will take you in
despite all too familiar plots,
deep reservations.

Her love, her life and death
come from the same place
without shame

or the bullshit of strangers
who mutter softly in the dark
and threaten to take over.

Ⅱ
Gemini
It's not that they don't wake every morning
heads full of thunderhooves, cannonballs,
screams of the wounded and dying,
it's as if their twinned souls fight,
invade territories inhabited by terrorists
who come out after dark making the city unsafe.

It's not that they don't sit in the window,
gazing over unfootprinted dew
but no one introduced them
to love – if it was love
that brought them to this –
face against glass. Waiting.

It's not that they won't drink
but their tea tastes of undusted corners,
unmade beds, unopened closets
and, cold cup in hand, they hear words
no one here has ever spoken
in this room.

♋

Cancer
           Out-of-season woman,
you slow and surely side-step

uncultivated shores –
then skinny-dip.

You take the kick-sand-in-the-eye
sentiment of old photos,

wearing faces
you claim to have loved

(or will learn how to love
in some other country)

into a distant timeframe – then,
when you are old

and careless,
you'll say you are sorry

when you no longer need
to explain.

Leo

Listen for the footpads of summer,
the soft cough that chips a hole
in suburban silence, the heavy
breathing, shift of weight,

shiver of skin (pelt) between
the green of leaf and shadow
as small summer munchers
turn multi-focused eyes to light,

to the sound of screen doors slamming,
wheels whispering
over dew-wet pavement,

of lions
licking their paws
underneath the back porch,

the man
across the street
laughing.

♍
Virgo

It was all those fill-in-the-blank days
she had to live through. Calendar
scrawls – birthdays, holidays, work

shop
every other Wednesday, church
on Sunday, bridge...

a facsimile
self
moves in, takes over – she suspects

soul does not exist, nothing diminishes
pain or pleasure,
gives it permanence.

Clouds scrape the sky,
pale stars (in their dotage)
stare down, pitiless.

Death
is much too busy keeping score
to be the right answer.

♎︎
Libra   Yellow eyes shine through twilight,
sullen and insatiable
as unslept shadows.

This is the children's hour
where good guy meets bad guy
and nobody wins or loses.

They want to play in the dark,
with danger,
with the promise of death

until they learn
how easy it comes, how hard
it is to live

and how beautiful.

♏
Scorpio

A small girl limps
across the narrow street,
recrosses,

her shrill cries
bounce off old redbrick
buildings,

break open the windows
of the still-asleep (the worn-out,
the walking wounded). Some women

have visible scars, wear
them like medals won
for survival, acquire them

like tattoos
for street-cred. Some women
quickshift

from being too young to matter
to being too old
to care.

↗
Sagittarius He's a big shot, high strung,
impervious to cold, tight-fisted strangers,

listens to the sea's white applause,
the earth's dim scream –

deaf as any lover to reality,
mouth sulky with brandy,

words remain only that.
But he holds on –

hands bruised, bleeding –
you can't leave him with his fear.

And the years pass, voices falter,
hands grow hard, callused.

He needs you here – needs someone to cry
when he dies.

♑
Capricorn

Empty days build into memory,
a gaol for hate, birthblood
stale in the mind, rank and inflexible.

Love and slow selfblame, grief
whimpers and stares.
The past brings no utterances,

no eyes overflowing. It is only now,
down the long tunnel of time,
you see the innocence

no one can touch or take from her.
It is with the obstinacy of a child
she clings to Sunday – before the rain.

Leave her
her yesterday. Leave her
alone.

Aquarius

From dead-centre you see the eye of the hurricane.
The air solid under ice – all day and night
you wait for someone to tell you the secret,
tell you what's really going on.

To be on the topmost floor in the dead of night
wondering if you are good enough,
smart enough, beautiful...
you only know that you survived,

or think you did. You licked the honey-pot,
tasted everything but death – now you've studied it,
have spoken it fluently
a year or more.

♓
Pisces

We do all we can to maintain our love –
hold tight to small scraps of beauty,
forgive bad behaviour,

push into the morningrush of cars,
into the bright, brash,
beckoning street;

reach for pen and paper – make it beautiful,
                        make it real,
                        make it ours.

No good covering yourself with a condom
of irreproachable behaviour,
we are down here together

living
and, occasionally,
loving.

ACKNOWLEDGEMENTS

Becoming Familiar/Becoming New: *Poemata,* Vol. 21, No. 02,
June/Sept 2005 (Canada), *Frogmore Papers*, No. 67, Spring 2006
At Woodsgift: *Obsessed With Pipework*, 36 Autumn 2006,
Corcaigh: Weyfarers, No. 102, August 2007,*Ascent Aspirations,* Spring
2008 (Canada)
After a Poetry Reading at Tigh Filí: *The Ticking Crocodile*, 2004
Under An Amphibious Sun: *Purple Patch*, 113, March 2006
April and the Sun: *Reach* 120, April 2008
*On the First Sunday After the First Full Moon After the Vernal
Equinox*: *Reach* 63, Nov. 2002
Alive,Alive Oh!: *Aireings*, No. 42, 2001
You Can Almost Hear Their Voices: *Mslexia*, Issue 40 Jan-Mar '09
Again: *Reach*, 106 Sept/Oct 2006, Ascent Aspirations, 2005 (Canada)
Pianissimo: *Peterloo Poetry* Anthology 2008, *Mothers and Daughters,*
Vol 10, No. 2 Fall Winter 2008 (Canada)
Sing to the Child: *Frogmore Papers,* No. 51, March 1998
Trad Music Night at Sin É: *Poetry Monthly*, Issue 112, July 2005
One Per Person: *The SHOp*, Issue No. 25, Autumn/Winter 2007
(Ireland)
The Opposite of Truth: *Pennine Platform*, No. 61 2007
After the Angelus: *Tower,* Vol. 54, No.2, Winter 2005/06 (Canada)
Outward and Visible Signs: *The Antigonish Review*, Issue 155, Autumn
2008 (Canada)
After Columbus: *FIRM noncommittal*, No.5, Summer 1999
This Island: *FIRE* , 15, Sept 2001, *boho press anthology*, 2004
A Red Sun Burns: *Poetry Nottingham*, Vol. 55, No.4, Winter 2001
Steel Drums: *Poetry Nottingham*, Vol. 55, No.4, Winter 2001
If You Stand: *Sepia*, 69, Sept 2002
The Big Empty: *The Stinging Fly*, Summer 2005 (Ireland)
Blackskinned Tropical Nights: *FIRE*, No.4, September 1997
And You Sleep: *The Journal*, #15, Spring 2006
Before: *Reach*, 102, April 2006, *Borderless Sky/Cielo sin fronteeras,*
2007 (Canada/Cuba)

An Appearance of Pelicans: *Pennine Platform*, No. 62, 2007
A Pelican Sky: *FreeFall*, Vol.XIV, No. 2, Fall, 2004 (Canada) *Borderless Sky/Cielo sin fronteras*, 2007 (Canada/Cuba)
George Town in the Rain: *Listening to the birth of crystals*, 2004
Wet: *Inclement*, Vol.1, Issue 5, 2001
Under the Meniscus: *Tears in the Fence*, No.37, Spring 2004,*Open Window*, IV, 2005 (Canada)
Seven Days and Six Nights Out of Context: *The Journal*, #24, Winter 2008/09
In Our House: *Purple Patch*, Issue 113, March 2006
To Whom It May Concern: *Obsessed With Pipework*, 36, Autumn 2006
Every House has a Room That Doesn't Exist: *Tears in the Fence*, 48, Autumn 2008
What You Learn in the Dark: *The Interpreter's House*, 31, Feb. 2006
After the Last Funeral: *South*, 39, April 2009
In a Second: *Orbis*, 127, Winter 2003
Been There: *Acumen*, 55, May 2006
And Peace Is: *The SHOp*, Issue No.20, Summer 2006 (Ireland)
Flying Without You: *The Journal*, #27. Summer 2009
Midafternoon: *The Stinging Fly*, issue 6, Vol. 2, Spring 2007 (Ireland)
A Woman Can: *Poemata*, Vol. 15, No.5, Sept/Oct 1999 (Canada), *And no one knows the blood we share*, 2005 (Canada)
And She's Gone Where So Many Children Have Gone: *Envoi*, 142, Oct. 2005
Caught In Her Throat Like the Words of a Mother: *Envoi*,142,Oct.'05
As Finding the Enemy Dressed as Love: *Envoi*, 142, Oct. 2005
And Once Again: *Southword*, 13, December 2007 (Ireland)
Pale Stars in their Dotage: *Hub City*, #3, 2000 (Canada), *Echoes of Gilgamesh*, October 2004

Indigo Dreams Publishing
132, Hinckley Road
Stoney Stanton
Leicestershire
LE9 4LN
www.indigodreamsonline.com